MONEY BOX

Saving Money

Ben Hubbard

and Beatriz Castro

W

FRANKLIN WATTS

LONDON • SYDNEY

First published in Great Britain in 2019 by
The Watts Publishing Group
Copyright © The Watts Publishing
Group 2019

Credits
Series Editor: Julia Bird
Illustrator: Beatriz Castro
Packaged by: Collaborate

HB ISBN 978 1 4451 6438 0
PB ISBN 978 1 4451 6439 7

Franklin Watts
An imprint of
Hachette Children's Group
Part of The Watts Publishing Group
Carmelite House
50 Victoria Embankment
London EC4Y 0DZ

An Hachette UK Company
www.hachette.co.uk
www.franklinwatts.co.uk

Printed in Dubai

MONEY BOX

Saving Money

This book is all about money. Why is money important? You can't eat or drink it, but most of us need money to survive. We use money to pay for nearly everything: clothes, electricity, food and water. It is hard to imagine a world without money.

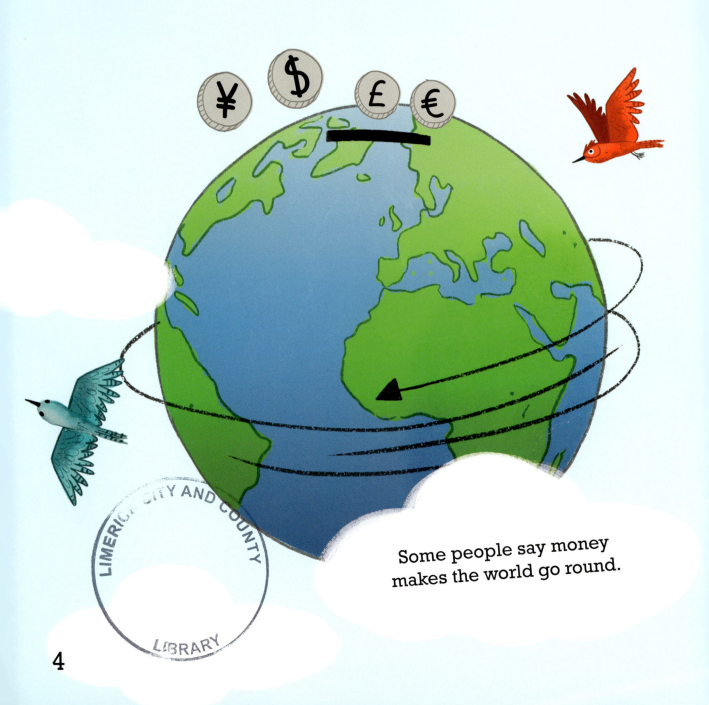

Some people say money makes the world go round.

When we have some money, we have to make choices.
What should we do with our money? We can:

Save it

Spend it

Share it

Or, make more money!

In the following pages, Marek tries to save some money. Keep reading to see if he can!

Every week, Marek's parents give him some pocket money. He doesn't spend much of it. Instead, Marek stuffs most of the money into his piggy bank.

After school, Marek has his friend Amanda over. Amanda doesn't have to do any chores for her pocket money. She also spends all of her pocket money very quickly!

Amanda says Marek should empty his piggy bank. Marek isn't sure, but in the end he agrees.

Wow, look at all that money!

Let's go to the corner shop!

The friends buy a big pile of sweets and cakes and eat far too much. Soon afterwards, they both feel a bit sick.

How much did we spend?

Four weeks' worth of your pocket money.

After Amanda went home Marek lay on the sofa watching TV. He still felt sick from the sweets and upset about all the money he spent.

More people than ever are suffering from buyer's remorse. This means feeling bad, guilty or regretful about a purchase.

The next day, Marek is still upset.
He can't believe he wasted so much
of his money on sweets. His dad
tries to make him feel better.

I could have put that
money towards a new
kick scooter.

Don't worry, you still
have some money
left. And you can start
saving again.

To help Marek with his money, his dad gets two empty jars.
They write 'savings' on one and 'spending' on the other.

After a few weeks, Marek finds he enjoys saving his pocket money and watching it grow. His mum helps him draw up a savings chart for his wall. As Marek saves, he fills in the space to his target – a new kick scooter.

A plan for saving and spending your money is called a budget.

Marek is saving most of his pocket money, but his chart is growing too slowly. Luckily, his family have some paying jobs he can do.

Marek is exhausted after finishing his jobs. But he also has a lot more money. His savings jar is filling up fast. So is his savings chart.

After school, Marek's mum takes him to the bank. Here, he will open his own savings account. This will replace the savings jar Marek has at home.

Here's your banking book, and you can also look at your account online.

We'll put half your pocket money into your account by direct debit and give you the other half in cash.

Yes, that's the half for my spending jar!

The bank teller shows Marek that his savings account has an interest rate. This means he gets some extra money for the savings he keeps there. The more savings he has, the more interest he gets.

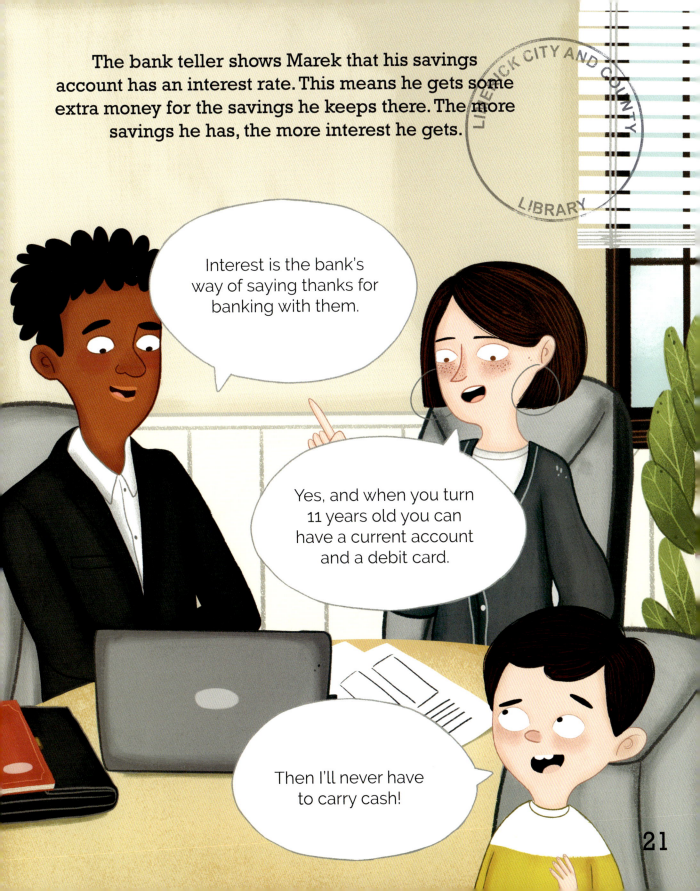

Interest is the bank's way of saying thanks for banking with them.

Yes, and when you turn 11 years old you can have a current account and a debit card.

Then I'll never have to carry cash!

After a few weeks of saving, Marek decides to reward himself. He takes some money out of his spending jar and buys a T-shirt he likes.

All the kids are wearing these at the ramp.

It's your money Marek!

Marek likes his new T-shirt, but for some reason it doesn't keep him happy for long. He finds himself looking at more clothes to buy online.

I thought one T-shirt would be enough, but now I want more. Why?

Buying things gives you a quick buzz, but then it wears off. Then you feel like buying more things to get the buzz back! Come on – let's go play in the park instead.

After talking to his sister, Marek decides not to spend any more money on clothes. Instead, he will save all of his pocket money until he reaches his kick scooter target.

£80

70

60

50

40

30

20

10

MAREK'S SAVINGS CHART

SPENDING SAVINGS

Marek has learnt a great lesson about money: it can't buy you happiness. The most fun he had in ages was playing in the park with his sister. Together they write a list of their favourite things that don't cost money.

Grandad always says the best things in life are free.

BEING WITH FAMILY
Swimming in the sea
Reading
RIDING KICK SCOOTERS
TALKING TO MY MATES
SCARING MY SISTER!
Having a bath after getting wet
EATING IN BED
Playing cards with Mum and Dad

It's a great day today! Marek has reached his target to buy his kick scooter. Together he and his dad order the scooter.

I'll show you how to buy the scooter online.

It even has next-day delivery!

The next day Marek waits patiently by the door for his scooter to arrive. And then…

It's here!

27

Marek loves his new scooter. It's fun to hang out with his friends at the skatepark and learn the latest tricks. However, the best part wasn't buying the scooter – it was saving up for it. It was really satisfying to set himself a goal and then reach it.

Quiz

Now you've reached the end of the book, how much do you think you've learned about saving money? Take this test to find out.

1 Where do some people keep their money?
- a   A piggy farm
- b   A piggy bank
- c   A piggy bowl

2 What is pocket money?
- a   Money you keep in your pocket
- b   Money your parents give you, often in return for doing chores
- c   Money with pockets printed on it

3 Which of these is a common bank card?
- a   Haveit card
- b   Cashout card
- c   Debit card

4 What is an interest rate?
- a   Extra money for keeping savings at a bank
- b   Extra money that comes in interesting shapes
- c   Extra money people pay the government

5 Where do people often do their banking?
- a   Online
- b   On a boat
- c   On a banking bus

Answers
b, b, c, a, a

Money words

Budget
A plan for your money.

Buyer's remorse
When you feel bad after buying something, and regret your decision.

Current account
An arrangement with a bank where you give them your money to look after, and can take the money out when you need it.

Debit card
A plastic card that your bank gives you to take out money from your account or pay for purchases in shops or online.

Direct debit
An instruction to your bank to make a regular payment to a company or organisation from your account.

Pocket money
Money that some children are given by their parents, usually for help with doing household chores.

Savings account
A bank account that adds money, called interest, to the money you have saved in the account.

Money facts

There's always more to learn about money.
Check out these facts!

- Because paper money moves between people, it often picks up germs. Remember to wash your hands after handling it!

- The first credit card was called the Diners Card. It was invented by Frank McNamara after he forgot to bring his wallet to a restaurant in 1949.

- For a period of time spices were worth more than gold in medieval Europe (c.500-1500).

- In 1999, 11 European countries made the Euro their currency.

- Governments get their money in three ways: they make it, borrow it from other countries and collect it from people through taxation.

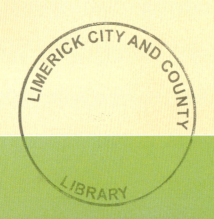